Basketball's MVPs

Jugadores más valiosos del baloncesto

Dan Osier

KEVIN GARNETT

PowerKiDS
press.

New York

Published in 2011 by The Rosen Publishing Group, Inc.
29 East 21st Street, New York, NY 10010

First Edition

Editor: Amelie von Zumbusch
Book Design: Kate Laczynski
Traducción al español: Eduardo Alamán

Photo Credits: Cover, p. 1 Paul J. Richards/AFP/Getty Images; p. 4 Gregory Shamus/Getty Images; pp. 6–7 Brian Babineau/NBAE/ Getty Images; p. 8 Amanda Edwards/Getty Images; p. 11 David E. Klutho/Getty Images; p. 12 Andy Hayt/NBAE/Getty Images; p. 15 David Sherman/NBAE/Getty Images; pp. 16–17 Jesse D. Garrabrant/Getty Images; p. 19 John Gichigi/Getty Images; p. 20 Kevin C. Cox/Getty Images; p. 22 Ronald Martinez/Getty Images.

Library of Congress Cataloging-in-Publication Data
Osier, Dan.
  Kevin Garnett / by Dan Osier. — 1st ed.
      p. cm. — (Basketball's MVPs / Jugadores más valiosos del baloncesto)
Text in English and Spanish.
Includes index.
ISBN 978-1-4488-3206-4 (library binding)
1. Garnett, Kevin, 1976- 2. Basketball players—United States— Biography. I. Title.
GV884.G3O85 2011
796.323092—dc22
[B]
                              2010026547

Manufactured in the United States of America

CPSIA Compliance Information: Batch #WW11PK: For Further Information contact Rosen Publishing, New York, New York at 1-800-237-9932

CONTENTS

CONTENIDO

This is Kevin Garnett. His nickname is The Big Ticket.

Éste es Kevin Garnett. Garnett es conocido como "La gran atracción."

Garnett plays power forward. He has **scored** more than 20,000 points over the years.

Garnett juega como alero. Garnett ha **anotado** más de 20,000 puntos en su carrera.

8

Kevin Garnett was born and grew up in South Carolina. He was born on May 19, 1976.

Kevin Garnett nació en Carolina del Sur. Garnet nació el 19 de mayo de 1976.

In high school, Garnett was already a great player. After high school, he went right to the NBA.

Garnett fue un gran jugador desde la secundaria. Al acabar la secundaria se unió a la NBA.

Garnett joined the Minnesota Timberwolves in 1995. In 1996, he was named **Rookie** of the Year.

Garnett se unió a los Timberwolves de Minnesota en 1995. En 1996 fue nombrado **Novato** del Año.

Over the next few years, Garnett kept playing better. Soon he was a star and team leader.

Garnett continuó jugando muy bien. Muy pronto se convirtió en la estrella y líder del equipo.

16

In 2004, Garnell was named the NBA's most **valuable** player, or MVP.

En 2004, Garnett fue nombrado Jugador más **Valioso** de la NBA.

In 2007, Garnett was traded to the Boston Celtics. They wanted him to help them win a **championship**.

En 2007, Garnett se unió a los Celtics de Boston. Los Celtics querían ganar el **campeonato**.

19

Garnett played well with the Celtics. In 2008, the team won the NBA championship.

Garnett jugó muy bien con los Celtics. En 2008, el equipo ganó el campeonato de la NBA.

Garnett is a great player. He loves the game and works hard.

Garnett es un gran jugador que ama el baloncesto. Garnett trabaja arduamente.

BOOKS | LIBROS

Here are more books to read about Kevin Garnett and basketball:

Edwards, Ethan. *Meet Kevin Garnett: Basketball's Big Ticket*. All-Star Players. New York: PowerKids Press, 2008.

Fedorko, Jamie. *Kevin Garnett*. Overcoming Adversity: Sharing the American Dream. Broomall, PA: Mason Crest Publishers, 2009.

Bilingual Books:

Otten, Jack. *Baloncesto (Basketball) Entrenamiento deportivo*. New York: Editorial Buenas Letras, 2004.

WEB SITES | PÁGINAS DE INTERNET

Due to the changing nature of Internet links, PowerKids Press has developed an online list of Web sites related to the subject of this book. This site is updated regularly. Please use this link to access the list:
www.powerkidslinks.com/bmvp/kevinga/

GLOSSARY | GLOSARIO

championship (CHAM-pee-un-ship) A group of games played to decide the best, or the winner.

rookie (RU-kee) A new major-league player.

scored (SKAWRD) Made points in a game.

valuable (VAL-yoo-bul) Important.

anotar Hacer puntos en un partido.

campeonato (el) Un conjunto de partidos que se juegan para decidir cuál es el mejor.

novato (el) Un nuevo jugador de una liga.

valioso Importante.

INDEX | ÍNDICE